CENGAGE Learning

Novels for Students, Volume 20

Project Editors: Ira Mark Milne and Timothy Sisler **Editorial**: Anne Marie Hacht, Maikue Vang

Rights Acquisition and Management: Edna Hedblad, Sheila Spencer, Ann Taylor **Manufacturing**: Rhonda Williams

Imaging: Lezlie Light, Mike Logusz, Kelly A. Quin **Product Design**: Pamela A. E. Galbreath

Product Manager: Meggin Condino

© 2005 Thomson Gale, a part of the Thomson Corporation.

For more information, contact
Thomson Gale
27500 Drake Rd.
Farmington Hills, MI 48331-3535
Or you can visit our Internet site at

While every effort has been made to ensure the reliability of the information presented in this publication, Thomson Gale does not guarantee the accuracy of the data contained herein. Thomson Gale accepts no payment for listing; and inclusion in the publication of any organization, agency, institution, publication, service, or individual does not imply endorsement of the editors or publisher. Errors brought to the attention of the publisher and verified to the satisfaction of the publisher will be corrected in future editions.

ISBN 0-7876-6943-1
ISSN 1094-3552

Printed in the United States of America
10 9 8 7 6 5 4 3 2 1

Silas Marner

George Eliot

1861

Introduction

Silas Marner: The Weaver of Raveloe, by Victorian novelist George Eliot, was first published in 1861. The idea for the short novel, which she described as "a story of old-fashioned village life," came upon Eliot suddenly and interrupted her plans for the writing of another novel, *Romola*. After the publisher John Blackwood read some of the manuscript and told her he found it somber, Eliot replied that it was not a sad story because "it sets in a strong light the remedial influences of pure, natural human relations."

Silas Marner is a story of loss, alienation, and redemption that combines elements of fairy tale and myth with realism and humor. Set in the fictional village of Raveloe, it centers on Silas Marner, a weaver who is forced to leave his hometown in the north after being falsely accused of theft by members of his chapel. His religious faith gone, for fifteen years Marner isolates himself from the life of the village and becomes a miser. But when the gold that he cherishes is stolen, and he adopts a child whose mother has just died, his life changes dramatically for the better.

Silas Marner has always been admired as one of Eliot's best and most appealing works. Not only is it a touching story that ends, like the fairy tale, happily ever after, it also presents a realistic portrait of nineteenth-century life in a traditional English village in which the spirit of kindness and cooperation overrule petty differences.

Author Biography

George Eliot, neé Mary Ann Evans, was born on November 22, 1819, in Chilvers Coton, in Warwickshire, England, the daughter of estate manager Robert Evans and his wife Christiana Pearson. Evans was educated at home and at various schools, including Mrs. Wallington's school in Nuneaton, where she became an Evangelical Christian. When her mother died in 1836, Evans became her father's housekeeper, while continuing her education through private tutors. She learned Italian, German, and Latin, and within a few years also studied Greek and Hebrew.

In 1841, Evans and her father moved to the outskirts of Coventry. There she met the philanthropist Charles Bray and his wife, Caroline Hennell, as well as Hennell's family, who introduced her to new political and religious ideas and under whose influence she rejected Christianity.

Evans translated and published David Friedrich Strauss's *The Life of Jesus* in 1846, and within three years she had also translated the work of the philosophers Spinoza and Feuerbach. After her father died in 1849, she moved to London and became assistant editor of the influential journal, *Westminster Review*. In the London literary circles in which she now moved, she met the man of letters, essayist and playwright, George Henry Lewes, and in 1853 she traveled to Germany with him. Lewes was estranged from his wife but was unable to obtain a divorce, and he and Evans lived together until Lewes's death in 1878. Their relationship shocked Victorian society; even Evans's brother Isaac refused to communicate with her in any way until after Lewes's death.

While Evans experienced social isolation because of her relationship with Lewes, she excelled as a novelist. In 1857, she published her first work of fiction, "The Sad Fortunes of the Reverend Amos Barton," in *Blackwood's Magazine*, under the pseudonym George Eliot, the name she used for all her subsequent works. The following year, "Amos Burton" was republished as one of Eliot's *Scenes of Clerical Life*, in two volumes.

Evans's first novel, *Adam Bede*, appeared in 1859, and achieved huge critical and popular success. Evans continued to maintain her anonymity, going to some lengths to disguise the fact that she was George Eliot. Over the next dozen years, Evans produced a series of novels that placed her in the front rank of English novelists. In 1860, after traveling with Lewes to Italy, she published *The Mill on the Floss*. *Silas Marner* followed in 1861, and *Romola*, a historical romance, was published in serial form in the *Cornhill* magazine in 1862 and 1863. It appeared in three volumes in 1863. *Felix Holt: The Radical* appeared in 1866, after which Evans and Lewes traveled extensively in Europe, visiting Holland, Belgium, Germany, and Spain. These European travels were a regular feature of Evans's life for the next decade.

Evans began writing her greatest novel, *Middlemarch*, in 1869. It was published in serial form from 1871 to 1872, and then in three volumes. Evans's last novel was *Daniel Deronda* (1876).

In 1880, two years after Lewes's death, Evans married John Walter Cross, who was twenty years her junior. She died that year, on December 22.

Plot Summary

Part 1

   Silas Marner begins in the early years of the nineteenth century, near the English village of Raveloe, where Silas Marner practices his trade as a weaver. He is a solitary man who is regarded as strange by the other villagers because he does not socialize with them. Marner first arrived in the village fifteen years earlier, from a large town in northern England. In his hometown he had lived a pious life and was a member of a Dissenting chapel (that is, a Protestant sect not affiliated to the Church of England) that met at Lantern Yard. But when Marner was falsely accused of theft by another member of the church, his friend William Dane, he was forced to leave the town and make his life elsewhere. With his religious faith shattered, Marner turned inward and made himself hard. Now, fifteen years later, the only thing he loves is his money, which he hoards.

   The chief family in Raveloe is that of Squire Cass. Cass has three sons, two of whom are important for the story. Dunsey, the youngest son is a dishonest ne'er-do-well, while Godfrey, the eldest, is good-natured but weak. Godfrey made the mistake of marrying secretly to Molly, a girl from a lower class. She became an opium addict and now threatens to betray his secret to his father. She also has a young child by Godfrey. Godfrey is terrified that his father will discover his secret and cut him off from his inheritance. He is also frustrated because he wants to marry Nancy Lammeter, a pretty girl from the village, but cannot do so as long as he is married to Molly. Dunsey knows his secret and blackmails him. Godfrey agrees to let Dunsey sell Godfrey's horse, Wildfire, to raise money, but Dunsey rides the horse foolishly, and it is killed in an accident. Dunsey walks home, and finding himself near Marner's cottage, he robs Marner, who has slipped out of his house on an errand, of all his gold. When Marner discovers the theft, he is distraught. Dunsey disappears, but no one connects his disappearance to the robbery. In the meantime, Marner's misfortune makes the villagers think more kindly of him.

On New Year's Eve, a dance is held at Red House, the home of Squire Cass. Molly decides to walk there to reveal the truth about Godfrey, but drugged on opium, she collapses near Marner's cottage. Her two-year-old daughter wanders into the cottage, where Marner discovers her asleep. Then Marner finds Molly and rushes to Red House for assistance, taking the child with him. When Molly is later declared dead, Marner insists on keeping the child, while Godfrey is relieved that the death of Molly leaves him free to marry Nancy Lammeter. He also goes out of his way to show kindness to Marner and the child, who is his daughter.

Marner christens the child Eppie and raises her as his own. The presence of the child revives his

Characters

Dunstan Cass

Dunstan Cass is Godfrey's younger brother. He is a disreputable, dishonest, spiteful young man who uses his knowledge of Godfrey's secret marriage to blackmail him. Godfrey agrees to let Dunsey sell Godfrey's horse, Wildfire, to raise money, but Dunsey rides the horse foolishly and is responsible for the horse's death. As he walks home, Dunsey robs Marner of his gold and then disappears. No one is concerned by his absence, since he has left home for long periods before. His remains are discovered sixteen years later in a stone-pit that has gone dry. It is concluded that he drowned.

Godfrey Cass

Godfrey Cass is the eldest son of Squire Cass and heir to the estate. He is a good-natured man, but he lacks strength of character and does not like to face up to difficult situations. In a fit of drunkenness he made the mistake of marrying beneath his station, and he has kept his wife and child a secret. He lives in fear that his ill-willed younger brother Dunsey will tell their father about his secret, which would probably result in his being turned out of the family home and cut off from his inheritance. He is also bitterly frustrated by the fact that because he is already married, he cannot marry the girl of his choice, Nancy Lammeter. When his wife dies and Dunsey disappears, Godfrey's worries appear to be over, and he duly marries Nancy. But he is tormented by the fact that his unacknowledged daughter Eppie is being raised by Marner. He shows as much care and concern for her as he can without arousing suspicion, and he tries to persuade Nancy that they should adopt Eppie. But Nancy refuses. After Dunsey's remains are found, Godfrey tells Nancy everything about his past. They try to adopt Eppie, but she refuses to be parted from the man she regards as her father. Godfrey is forced to accept that he can never publicly acknowledge Eppie as his daughter, a blow for which his happy marriage is only partial consolation.

Molly Cass

Molly Cass is Godfrey Cass's first wife, whom he married secretly. She comes from a lower social class than her husband, and she is addicted to opium. She decides to walk to the Red House on New Year's Eve to betray Godfrey's secret, but she collapses and dies near Marner's cottage.

Squire Cass

Squire Cass, the father of Dunsey and Godfrey, is the most prominent landowner in Raveloe. A widower of sixty, he is a bluff, robust, quick-tempered man who never questions the superiority of his own family within the parish. He is a difficult man to deal with. He is indulgent with his tenants for a while and lets them get into arrears, but then when he gets short of money, he comes down on them hard for rent. Once he has made up his mind about something, he does not alter it.

William Dane

William Dane is a treacherous friend of Silas. When they are both young men, they are devout members of a religious sect that meets at Lantern Yard in a town in northern England. But Dane steals money from the church and deliberately arranges for Marner to take the blame. He then marries the girl to whom Marner had been engaged.

Dunsey

See Dunstan Cass

Eppie

Eppie is the daughter of Godfrey and Molly Cass. Since Godfrey will not acknowledge his marriage, it is left to Molly to raise the child. But she is unfit to do so, and when she dies of an overdose of opium, the child is adopted by Marner. He christens her Eppie. Eppie grows up in a loving home and regards Marner as her father. She is pretty, with golden curly hair. She is content with her position in life and has no interest in being adopted by Godfrey and Nancy, even when she is informed that Godfrey is her real father. She remains utterly loyal and devoted to Marner and is happy to be associated with the poor, working people of the village. When she is eighteen, Eppie marries Aaron, and they live together in Marner's cottage.

Mr. Kimble

Mr. Kimble is the village farrier (veterinarian), and he also serves as the town doctor. Because of his status he has a rather high opinion of himself. It is Kimble who takes charge of the situation in the Rainbow tavern after Marner tells the people he has been robbed.

Nancy Lammeter

Nancy Lammeter is the attractive young woman courted by Godfrey Cass. Nancy is well mannered, sincere, and always neat; at the New Year's Eve dance she is perfectly attired, with not a hair out of place. Although Nancy is a woman of good character, she also lives by some rigid, simple ideas, which she refuses to alter. She insists that her sister Priscilla dress in exactly the same way as she does, even though this does not set Priscilla off to best advantage. Nancy also refuses to adopt Eppie, even though Godfrey her husband greatly desires it, because she believes that Providence has decreed she remain childless. In Nancy's inflexible mind, adopting a child would be wrong, and the child would not turn out well. In spite of this fault, however, Nancy is a good, tender wife to Godfrey, and after he finally confesses his past indiscretions she agrees to try to adopt Eppie.

Priscilla Lammeter

Priscilla Lammeter is Nancy Lammeter's sister. Five years older than Nancy, she is not as pretty as her sister and describes herself as ugly. But she does not seem to mind this disadvantage. She is a cheerful woman, full of common sense, and she has no wish to marry.

Mr. Macey

Mr. Macey is the old tailor and parish clerk of Raveloe. He often tells stories about village history in the Rainbow, and the men listen to him with respect.

Silas Marner

Silas Marner is a weaver. As a young man living in a town in northern England, he is a member of a fundamentalist Christian sect that meets at a place called Lantern Yard. He is highly thought of by the other members of the sect, and the fact that during prayer meetings he sometimes goes into trances that last as long as an hour is seen as a sign of some special spiritual gift. But Marner is driven away from the town after his treacherous friend, William Dane, ensures that Marner is falsely convicted of theft. Marner settles in Raveloe, but his faith is shattered, and he isolates himself from the community. The villagers regard him with suspicion, which is not helped by the fact that Marner has knowledge of the healing properties of herbs. The superstitious villagers think this kind of knowledge may have something to do with the devil. Marner does not attend church and knows nothing of the village's church calendar because it is very different from the sect of Christianity practiced in Lantern Yard. The only thing he loves is his money. He earns a good income as a weaver, working alone in his cottage, and he hoards his gold, counting it lovingly. When the gold is stolen he is shattered. He seeks help from the villagers, and they begin to think more kindly of him. Marner's life changes completely when a child whose mother lies dead in the snow near his home finds her way to his cottage. He insists on raising her himself. The child, christened Eppie, brings out Marner's latent kindness and gentleness. Through Eppie he realizes that love is more valuable than money. He is then able to connect with the life of the community, and he becomes a respected and honored citizen of Raveloe.

Mr. Tookey

Mr. Tookey is the deputy parish clerk and is unpopular with the other men.

Aaron Winthrop

Aaron Winthrop is the son of Dolly Winthrop. He is a steady, good-hearted young man, and he marries Eppie while promising also to take care of

Marner.

Dolly Winthrop

Dolly Winthrop is the mother of Aaron and the wife of Ben, the village wheelwright. She is a mild, patient, hard-working woman who is always ready to look after the sick and the dying. She is one of the first of the villagers to take pity on Marner after his gold has been stolen, visiting him with her young son and bringing lard-cakes. Dolly supports Marner's decision to adopt Eppie, and she is full of valuable advice and practical help about how to raise the child.

Themes

Moral Order

Although there are tragedies in *Silas Marner* (the death of Molly Cass, for example), the narrative emphasizes the moral order of the universe. The principal characters get their just desserts. Silas Marner is rewarded for the love he shows Eppie; Dunsey never lives to profit from his robbery; and Godfrey Cass, because of his deceitfulness and moral cowardice, can never publicly acknowledge that Eppie is his daughter. This moral order is at work through seemingly chance events. It seems to be chance, for example, that Marner happens to be away from his cottage on a short errand and has left his door unlocked (which he would never normally do) at the exact moment that Dunsey is walking by, thus giving Dunsey a chance to rob him. It also seems to be a chance event when Molly Cass collapses near Marner's cottage and Eppie wanders inside. The door to the cottage is once again open and Marner is in one of his strange trances, so he does not notice the girl until she is asleep on his hearth.

But there is more at work than chance. Almost as soon as he sees the child, Marner senses that some supernatural order is operating in his life, and he later thinks that the child must have been deliberately sent to him. Dolly Winthrop agrees with him, although neither offers any explanation as to who or what this benevolent power might be. Later, after Marner has explained his past life to Dolly, she struggles to articulate her intuitive feeling that there is a higher power that arranges everything for the best: "For if us as knows so little can see a bit o' good and rights, we may be sure as there's a good and a rights bigger nor what we can know."

The Need for Human Community

The novel presents pictures of two poles of human existence, isolation and community. For fifteen years Marner retreats into a solitude that denies life. He is redeemed only when events conspire to make him rejoin a human community.

In his years of isolation at Raveloe, cut off from the real springs of life, Marner makes the mistake of treating inert things as if they were alive. His delight in his gold is so great that it even gratifies his senses of touch and sight: "It was pleasant to feel them [the guineas] in his palm"; he enjoys looking at their "bright faces"; they offer him "companionship," and as he "bathed his hands" in them he "felt their rounded outline between his thumb and fingers." He even begins to think that the gold is conscious of him, as he believes his loom is. And Marner's life, with its ceaseless, monotonous, repetitive activity, has come to resemble the actions of the loom. His constant bending over his loom has also deformed him physically, making him curiously fitted to it, like a "handle or a crooked tube" that has no independent existence apart from what it is attached to. In his attachment to a machine, Marner has cut himself off from nature. He forgets all about his former interest in herbs and his skill in using them for healing. When he walks through the lanes on a work-related trip, he thinks only of his money and his loom. The life of nature goes on around him unobserved. As a miser, he has given to inanimate things a spurious life and forgotten what real life is. His own life has become "a mere pulsation of desire and satisfaction that had no relation to any other being."

Topics for Further Study

- Does Godfrey Cass, Eppie's biological father, have the right to take her from Silas Marner, her foster father? What moral issues does this matter raise? How is this issue relevant in the early 2000s?

- Bearing in mind that Eliot has sometimes been criticized by feminists for being too conservative in her representation of women, discuss the characters Nancy Lammeter, Dolly Winthrop, and Eppie. Are they presented as dependent on men? How do they go about fulfilling their needs and desires? How do they support others?

- Discuss how Silas Marner rears Eppie. What principles does he follow? Does he follow Dolly Winthrop's advice? What role does punishment have in childrearing?

- Write a detailed analysis of the scene in Chapter 6 in which the male villagers meet at the Rainbow. Who are the main characters, and what do they discuss? What does this scene reveal about village life in Raveloe? Why is the scene placed at this point in the narrative?

The loss of his money is a blessing in disguise for Marner because it breaks his attachment to things that have no life. It also reveals that the human spirit within him is not quite dead. He has a dim sense that if any help is to reach him, it must come from outside. This is why, when the villagers become more sympathetic to him, "there was a slight stirring of expectation at the sight of his fellow-men, a faint consciousness of dependence on their goodwill." This faint channel of hope is symbolized by the fact that at Christmas, Marner, even though he is still full of grief, does not make any attempt to close the shutters or lock the door of his cottage. Moreover, he develops a habit of opening his door and looking out from time to time. He does this not because he is consciously inviting companionship, but because he has some irrational hope that his money will somehow be returned. But it is this habit of leaving his door open that allows the child to come into his life. It is a sign that he has begun his journey back from isolation to community.

The arrival of Eppie has an immediate effect on Marner. When he first sees the child, he thinks it may be his little sister, come back in a dream. He remembers how he carried his sister around in his arms for a year until she died. By recalling a tender time of childhood that he had closed off from memory, Silas begins the process of reconnecting with his past. The process continues when he tells Dolly Winthrop all the details of his early life. Through this process his fractured psyche starts to become whole again. And with Eppie taking his thoughts away from their endless circularity into a more outward direction, Marner is at last ready to become integrated into the community life of Raveloe.

Just as Marner is a case study in isolation, Raveloe is presented as an example of community. There are two centers of community in Raveloe: the Squire's Red House, which is generous in giving out food to the poor and hosts the New Year's Eve dance, and the Rainbow inn, where the villagers gather round the hearth to tell their stories. The inhabitants of Raveloe may not be perfect, but they are fairly easy going and do not make a habit of applying moral censure to others. Although the village is strictly divided along class lines, there is no envy of the rich by the poor. It is a community in which everyone knows his or her place, and a spirit of cooperation and tolerance is the norm. This is shown especially vividly when the men in the Rainbow immediately do everything they can to help Marner, a man they all regard as rather strange, when he informs them that he has been robbed. The villagers all know that they are dependent on each other, and when Marner also realizes this, he is ready to play his part in a wider community, instead of foolishly trying to be self-sufficient.

Imagery

In becoming a solitary miser, Silas Marner has become almost less than human, a point which is brought out by the imagery that is associated with him. He is described as like a spider, weaving its web; his life is reduced to the "unquestioning activity of a spinning insect." After he has lost his money, the image changes to that of an ant. His mind is baffled like a "plodding ant" that on its way home finds that the earth has been moved.

The imagery changes when Marner is on the way to redemption. When he sits with Eppie on a bank of flowers listening to the birds, he starts to look for herbs again, as he did when he was younger. As a leaf lies in his palm, memories of the past come flooding back to him. His mind is "growing into memory," and his soul is "unfolding too, and trembling gradually into full consciousness." Instead of being compared to an insect, Marner is now implicitly likened to an unfolding flower.

Fairy Tale and Realism

The narrative combines elements of the fairy tale with realistic settings and characters. Fairy tales often tell of a man or woman who is unjustly banished from a kingdom or is otherwise the victim of great misfortune. The person then goes through many trials and much suffering and feels that all is lost. Chance events, often involving the supernatural, intervene, evil is punished, good is rewarded, a perfect marriage is arranged, and the characters live happily ever after.

The story of Silas Marner has clear affinities with the fairy tale. Silas is unjustly expelled from his hometown and arrives in what is to him an alien environment. As a miser hoarding his gold, he is like a stock figure in folklore and fairy tale. When the miser sees the child and mistakes her golden curls for his stolen gold, the narrative is firmly in fairy tale mode. Marner's restoration to happiness and the happy ending with Eppie marrying Aaron are also strongly reminiscent of the fairy tale.

But other elements in the story are realistic. Unlike fairy tales, which are set in unnamed places in unknown times, Silas Marner takes place at a definite time and in a definite place. It is anchored in rural England at the beginning of the nineteenth century. Village life and customs are described in realistic mode, and realism is also seen in the dialect in the villagers' speech. The story of Godfrey Cass, as opposed to that of the miser, contains no fairy tale elements. Godfrey's marriages, his family relations, the secret he keeps that may ruin him are the stuff of realistic Victorian fiction.

Compare & Contrast

- **1810s:** Each parish in England provides a workhouse to accommodate and employ the destitute. Conditions in the workhouses vary. Some are relatively acceptable, but others are grim. In 1810, George Crabbe writes of one workhouse: "It is a prison, with a milder name, / Which few inhabit without dread or shame."

1860s: Since the Poor Law Amendment Act of 1834, hundreds of new workhouses have been built. They are supervised by a local Board of Guardians. Conditions in the workhouses are intentionally made harsh and degrading, to deter all but the most desperate. They are inhabited mainly by the old, the infirm, the sick, the orphaned, and unmarried mothers. The largest of them house over a thousand people.

Today: Workhouses no longer exist. They were abolished in 1930. People who in addition to being poor are sick, old, or mentally ill are cared for in hospitals and by social welfare organizations. Under the National Health Service, every British citizen is entitled to free health care, according to his or her need. No social stigma is attached to being an unmarried mother, and women in such situations are able to gain employment.

- **1810s:** The population of England and Wales, according to the official census, is 10,164,000. The population is rising rapidly. The increase is due largely to a falling death rate, which falls from 33.4 per 1,000 in 1730 to 19.98 per 1,000 in 1810. This is due to better living conditions and better diet.

  1860s: The population continues to increase. There is a continuing shift of population to cities and away from rural areas. London is the biggest city in the world, with a population in 1861 of 2,803,989. This is an increase of 19 percent in ten years. Manchester also becomes one of the largest industrial centers in the world. After 1860, mortality rates decline because of the reduction in deaths from scarlet fever, typhus, and consumption.

  Today: The population of the United Kingdom (England, Scotland, Wales, and Northern Ireland) at mid-2001 is 58.8 million. Nearly 84 percent of this total lives in England, mainly in the major cities. London is the largest city in Europe, with a population of 7.2 million. The population of the

United Kingdom is increasing. It has risen by 10 million between 1950 and 2000, mainly due to rising immigration. The death rate has dropped to 10.35 deaths per 1,000 population.

- **1810s:** The Napoleonic Wars end in 1815. Britain's conservative government fears social revolution and represses civil liberties.

1860s: Britain increases democracy by extending the franchise. In the 1850s, only 900,000 out of 5,300,000 adult males in England and Wales were eligible to vote, but the Parliamentary Re-form Act of 1867 adds an additional 1,008,000 men to the voter rolls. An amendment for the enfranchisement of women is rejected by 196 to 73 votes in the House of Commons.

Today: Like all Western democracies, all British citizens who qualify by age are eligible to vote. However, voter participation is in decline. In the general election of 2001, only 59.4 percent of the total electorate vote. This figure is down from 70.9 percent in 1997 and 76.7 percent in 1992. It remains higher than voter turnout in the United States.

Weavers in England

Historian E. P. Thompson, in his book *The Making of the English Working Class*, describes four different employment situations for weavers during the nineteenth century. The first was the "customer-weaver," like Silas Marner, an independent worker in a village or small town who fulfilled orders from individual customers. Although customer-weavers were diminishing in numbers, those who continued the practice made a good living. In *Silas Marner*, Mr. Macey guesses that the hardworking Marner may make a pound a week from his weaving, which would have been a fairly sizable income. (This would have been during the early years of the nineteenth century.) The second kind of weaver was self-employed, producing work for a number of different masters. The third type was the journeyman weaver, who often owned his own loom and worked in his own home for one master. This was probably the status of Silas Marner in his hometown in northern England, where he learned his trade. The last category of weaver was the farmer who worked part-time at the loom. From 1780 to 1830, according to Thompson, these groups tended to merge into one group, "the proletarian outworker, who worked in his own home, sometimes owned and sometimes rented his loom, and who wove up the yarn to the specifications of the factor or agent of a mill or of some middleman."

Thompson emphasizes the loss of status and security that accompanied these changes, although weaving could still be a profitable business for the weaver.

The business was changing, however. The power loom was invented in 1784 and patented the following year. It enabled the weaver to once more to keep pace with the spinner, who up to then had been able to produce more yarn than the weaver could use. The power loom was first used in Manchester in 1791. By 1813, there were 2,400 power looms in England. But weaving remained predominantly a domestic industry until 1820, when power looms came into general use.

Social Change

At the beginning of the nineteenth century, England was a largely settled and static society. Villages like the fictional Raveloe in *Silas Marner* were relatively self-sufficient, since the inhabitants were able to manufacture their own clothes and supply their own food. But social change accelerated during the course of the century. Agricultural laborers and manufacturers became willing to leave villages in search of work or of better paid work. This was not just a matter of a shift from the countryside to the nearest town, but of large-scale migrations. By the end of the century, workers were moving to Lancashire, where the cotton industry was flourishing, at the rate of fifteen thousand a year. The town of Bolton, for example, increased its population from 5,339 in 1773 to 11,739 in 1789. New canals enabled raw materials to be transported more quickly and efficiently, and new roads facilitated the recruitment of a labor force. There was, however, a price to be paid for economic gain, and that was the creation of a new class of landless agricultural laborers, who had lost their independence.

By the beginning of the reign of King George IV in 1820, the huge growth in manufacturing towns that had little connection with the old rural communities had radically changed England. As social historian G. M. Trevelyan writes in *Illustrated English Social History*: "The harmonious fabric of old English society suffered a perpendicular cleavage between town and country, as well as expanding the old lateral cleavage between rich and poor."

Critical Overview

Although there have been occasional complaints that the first part of the book is too gloomy and the second part too sentimental, *Silas Marner* has always been highly regarded by literary critics. Initial reviews were all positive. In a review published in *The Times* in 1861, E. S. Dallas praised the novel for its truthful portrayal of village life. He pointed out that although the characters were not idealized they were given dignity by the author's treatment of them: The personages of the tale are common, very common people, but they are good and kind, hardworking and dutiful.... their lives are ennobled and beautified by their sense of duty, and by their sympathy with each other.

Many modern critics regard *Silas Marner* as a flawless work, although because it is only novella-length it is not regarded as Eliot's greatest novel. Critics have shown that the novel is far more than a simple moral tale about a miser who discovers through adopting a young child that love is more rewarding than money. Elizabeth Deeds Ermath analyzes the novel as a "double story about isolation and community," and points out the complex similarities and differences between the stories of Marner and Godfrey Cass. Q. D. Leavis, in her introduction to the Penguin edition of the novel, discusses it in terms of the social changes brought about by the Industrial Revolution. She points out that Marner, brought up in a manufacturing town, has become a slave to his loom—a piece of machinery—whereas Raveloe still clings to the traditional way of life, "the organic community and the unified society."

What Do I Read Next?

- Like *Silas Marner*, Eliot's novel *Adam Bede* (1859) is set in a fictional rural community in which the people adhere to traditional ways of communal living. Unlike the situation in *Silas Marner*, however, the villagers must learn to deal with the kinds of social change they are illequipped to face.

- *North and South* (1855), by Victorian novelist Elizabeth Gaskell, makes for an interesting comparison with Eliot's style and themes. Margaret Hale, a girl from southern

England, is unwillingly sent to the northern industrial city of Manchester, where she must adjust to a rougher society than the one in which she was raised.

- Frederick Robert Karl's biography *George Eliot: Voice of a Century: A Biography* (1995) has been widely praised for bringing Eliot vividly to life. Giving full attention to issues of class and gender, he recreates the world in which she lived and shows how she became a great writer.

- Asa Briggs's *The Age of Improvement: 1783–1867* (1959; 2d ed., 1999) is a classic study of how and why Britain changed from the time of the French Revolution to the mid-Victorian era. Briggs covers sociological, economic, political and cultural history.

- Richard Muir's *The English Village* (1980) describes the history of the English village and provides many photographs.

Sources

Dallas, E. S., Review of *Silas Marner*, in *The Critical Response to George Eliot*, edited by Karen L. Pangallo, Greenwood Press, 1994, pp. 94–96, originally published in *The Times*, April 29, 1861.

Eliot, George, *Silas Marner*, edited and with an introduction by Q. D. Leavis, Penguin, 1985.

Ermath, Elizabeth Deeds, *George Eliot*, Twayne's English Authors Series, No. 414, Twayne Publishers, 1985, pp. 97–102.

Leavis, Q. D., "Introduction," in *Silas Marner*, by George Eliot, edited by Q. D. Leavis, Penguin, 1985.

Thompson, E. P., *The Making of the English Working Class*, Penguin, 1968, pp. 297–346.

Trevelyan, G. M., *Illustrated English Social History*, Vol. 3, *The Eighteenth Century*, Harmondsworth, Penguin Books, 1968, p. 139.

Further Reading

Beer, Gillian, *George Eliot*, Indiana University Press, 1986, pp. 108–46.

> In this feminist study, Beer discusses Silas Marner, Romola, and Felix Holt in terms of the displacement involved in proposing a conflict between natural parents and nurturing parents.

Johnstone, Peggy Fitzburgh, *The Transformation of Rage: Mourning and Creativity in George Eliot's Fiction*, New York University Press, 1994, pp. 68–94.

> This is a Freudian interpretation of the novel, including a discussion of what is called obsessive-compulsive disorder (repetitious actions and thoughts) and its cure.

McCormack, Kathleen, *George Eliot and Intoxication: Dangerous Drugs for the Condition of England*, St. Martin's Press, 2000, pp. 91–109.

> As part of her study of Eliot's drug metaphors, McCormack analyzes the novel as a parable of addiction and recovery.

Speaight, Robert, Review of *Silas Marner*, in *George Eliot*, 2d ed., Arthur Barker, 1968, pp. 61–67.

This is a short review of the many outstanding aspects of the novel, including its characterization, its lack of excessive moralism, and its life-like realism that still allows for symbolic elements.